Looking at Animal Parts

Let's Look at Animal Ears

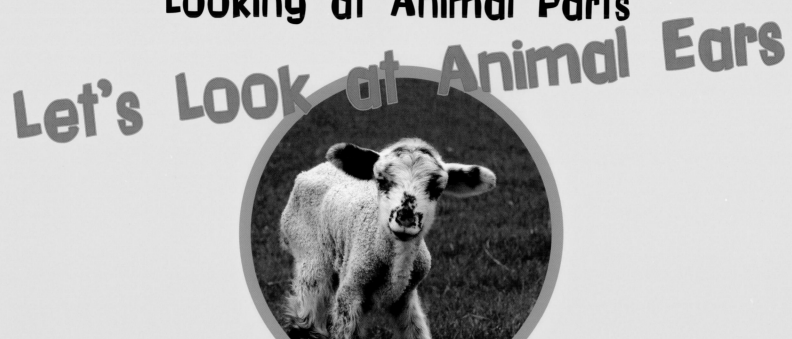

by Wendy Perkins

Consulting Editor: Gail Saunders-Smith, PhD

Consultant: Suzanne B. McLaren, Collections Manager
Section of Mammals, Carnegie Museum of Natural History
Edward O'Neil Research Center, Pittsburgh, Pennsylvania

Capstone
press

Mankato, Minnesota

Pebble Plus is published by Capstone Press,
151 Good Counsel Drive, P.O. Box 669, Mankato, Minnesota 56002.
www.capstonepress.com

1 2 3 4 5 6 11 10 09 08 07 06

Library of Congress Cataloging-in-Publication Data
Perkins, Wendy, 1957–
    Let's look at animal ears / by Wendy Perkins.
    p. cm.—(Pebble plus. Looking at animal parts)
    Summary: "Simple text and photographs present animal ears, how they work, and how different animals
use them"—Provided by publisher.
    Includes bibliographical references and index.
    ISBN-13: 978-0-7368-6348-3 (hardcover)
    ISBN-10: 0-7368-6348-6 (hardcover)
    1. Ear—Juvenile literature. I. Title. II. Series.
QL948.P45 2007
591.4′4—dc22
                                      2006000996

Editorial Credits
Sarah L. Schuette, editor; Kia Adams, set designer; Renée Doyle, cover production; Kelly Garvin, photo
    researcher/photo editor

Photo Credits
Brand X Pictures, cover
Capstone Press/Karon Dubke, 1
James P. Rowan, 18–19
McDonald Wildlife Photography/Joe McDonald, 17
Nature Picture Library/Graham Hatherley, 14–15; Larry Michael, 6–7; Laurent Geslin, 5; T. J. Rich, 12–13
Robert McCaw, 8–9
Shutterstock/Nicholas D. Cacchione, 11
Tom & Pat Leeson, 20–21

Note to Parents and Teachers

The Looking at Animal Parts set supports national science standards related to life
science. This book describes and illustrates animal ears. The images support early readers
in understanding the text. The repetition of words and phrases helps early readers learn
new words. This book also introduces early readers to subject-specific vocabulary words,
which are defined in the Glossary section. Early readers may need assistance to read
some words and to use the Table of Contents, Glossary, Read More, Internet Sites, and
Index sections of the book.

Table of Contents

Ears at Work

Animal ears pick up sounds.
Animals listen to what's
going on around them.

What's that?

A deer hears a sound

in the bushes.

It runs away.

A cougar hears the deer
and follows.
The deer becomes its prey.
Chomp!

Kinds of Ears

Cats turn their ears
from side to side.
They can tell where
sounds are coming from.

Gorillas turn their heads
to follow sounds.
Gorillas can't move their ears,
but they hear well.

Large ears help foxes listen
for food at night.
They can hear tiny mice
running across sand.

Long ears help jackrabbits
hear predators.
They hide by folding
their ears against their backs.

Bats have the best hearing

of all mammals.

They listen for echoes

from flying insects.

Awesome Animal Ears

Long or short,
flat or pointed,
animal ears pick up
all kinds of sounds.

Glossary

echo—a sound that repeats by bouncing off another object

insect—a small animal with a hard outer shell, six legs, three body sections, and two antennas; most insects have wings.

mammal—a warm-blooded animal with a backbone and hair or fur; female mammals feed milk to their young.

predator—an animal that hunts another animal for food

prey—an animal that is hunted for food

Read More

Arnold, Caroline. *Did You Hear That?: Animals with Super Hearing.* Watertown, Mass.: Charlesbridge, 2001.

Hall, Kirsten. *Animal Hearing.* Animals and Their Senses. Milwaukee: Weekly Reader Early Learning Library, 2005.

Hall, Peg. *Whose Ears Are These?: A Look at Animal Ears—Short, Flat, and Floppy.* Whose Is It? Minneapolis: Picture Window Books, 2003.

Internet Sites

FactHound offers a safe, fun way to find Internet sites related to this book. All of the sites on FactHound have been researched by our staff.

Here's how:

1. Visit *www.facthound.com*

2. Choose your grade level.

3. Type in this book ID **0736863486** for age-appropriate sites. You may also browse subjects by clicking on letters, or by clicking on pictures and words.

4. Click on the **Fetch It** button.

FactHound will fetch the best sites for you!

Index

Word Count: 132
Grade: 1
Early-Intervention Level: 14